Alain de Botton's

The Art of Travel

Study notes for Advanced English

Module C 2015–2020 HSC

Eleni Tatsis &
Lynne Slarke

A
FIVE SENSES
PUBLICATION

Five Senses Education Pty Ltd
2/195 Prospect Highway
Seven Hills 2147
New South Wales
Australia

First Published 2015

Tatsis, Eleni & Slarke, Lynne
Top Notes – The Art of Travel
ISBN 978-1-76032-001-0

2015.09.10

CONTENTS

TOP NOTES SERIES

This series has been created to assist HSC students of English in their understanding of set texts. Top Notes are easy to read, providing analysis of issues and discussion of important ideas contained in the texts.

Particular care has been taken to ensure that students are able to examine each text in the context of the module and elective to which it has been allocated.

Each text generally includes:

- Notes on the specific module
- Plot summary
- Character analysis
- Setting
- Thematic concerns
- Language studies
- Essay questions and a modelled response
- Other textual material
- Study practice questions
- Useful quotes

I am sure you will find these Top Notes useful in your studies of English.

Bruce Pattinson
Series Editor

THE ADVANCED COURSE

This is a brief overview of the Advanced course to ensure you are completely familiar with the different sections of the course. If in any doubt at all check with your teacher or the Board of Studies. The Board of Studies website is an excellent resource and information on the texts and course can be found at:

Board of Studies NSW HSC English Prescriptions 2015-2020

HTTP://WWW.BOARDOFSTUDIES.NSW.EDU.AU/SYLLABUS_HSC/ENGLISH/ENG-STD-ADV-PRESCRIPTIONS-2015-20.HTML

The Advanced Course requires you to have studied:

- Five prescribed texts. This means five texts from the list given to your teacher by the Board of Studies.
- For each of the texts, **one** must come from **each** of the following five categories.
    - Shakespearian drama
    - prose fiction (novel usually)
    - drama or film
    - poetry
    - non-fiction or media or film or multimedia texts. (Multimedia are CD Roms, websites, etc.)
- A range of related texts of your own choosing. These are part of your Area of Study: Discovery and Module C. Do not confuse these with the main set text you are studying and focusing on. This is very important.

Paper One

Area of Study: Discovery

Paper Two

Module A	*Module B*	*Module C*
Comparative Study of Texts and Context	**Critical Study of Text**	**Representation and Text**
Electives	▪ Prose Fiction OR ▪ Shakespeare OR ▪ Poetry OR ▪ Drama or Film OR ▪ Nonfiction, Media, Multimedia	***Electives***
▪ Intertextual Connections OR ▪ Intertextual Perspectives		▪ Representing People and Politics OR ▪ Representing People and Landscapes

You must study the Area of Study and EACH of Modules A, B and C

Module A and C Advanced have two electives. There are text options within EACH module. They are found on the Higher School Certificate Prescriptions List, 2015–20 which is published by the Board of Studies. This text is found within Elective 2, Representing People and Landscapes, in Module C.

THE RELEVANCE OF RUBRIC

It is vital that you understand the importance of the rubric and the module and elective structure. You do not only study a text or texts, you study them in relation to the elective and module in which they are placed. All questions derive from the module and elective structure so they should form the guidelines for your analysis of text.

Module C: Representation and Text

This module requires students to explore various representations of events, personalities or situations. They evaluate how medium of production, textual form, perspective and choice of language influence meaning. The study develops students' understanding of the relationships between representation and meaning. (Refer to the *English Stage 6 Syllabus*, p 48.)

Elective 2: Representing People and Landscapes

In this elective, students explore and evaluate various representations of people and landscapes in their prescribed text and other related texts of their own choosing. They consider the ways in which texts represent the relationship between the lives of individuals or groups and real, remembered or imagined landscapes. Students analyse representations of particular landscapes and their significance for the individual or society more broadly. In their responding and composing, students develop their understanding of how the relationship between various textual forms, media of production and language choices influences and shapes meaning.

How does the rubric relate to Alain de Botton's *The Art of Travel*?

For the purpose of this rubric, Alain de Botton 's *The Art of Travel* represents the various ways in which we, as people, interact with different types of landscapes. These landscapes may be encountered physically or imaginatively. The text represents characters' experiences of travelling in various landscapes. Characters include Alain de Botton as well as artists such as Edward Hopper and Vincent Van Gogh, writers like Charles Baudelaire and Gustave Flaubert, Renaissance men such as Edmund Burke and John Ruskin, and others including Alexander von Humboldt, the German explorer and William Wordsworth, the poet. De Botton's choice of genre, travelogue/self help, aims to persuade the reader through its collection of essays, that different types of landscapes have the ability to impact on our intellect, emotions and outlook on life.

How does the rubric relate to your related material?

Your selection of related material is up to you to locate and analyse. It could reveal similarities or differences in relation to your prescribed text. Some suggested related material is included in a section at the end of this book. It is also worth noting that Five Senses Education publishes a volume called *The Imaginative Landscape.*Several volumes of this book have been published for the Victorian equivalent of the HSC. You could find the texts outlined and analysed in these volumes invaluable for your related study of texts in this elective.

THE AUTHOR – ALAIN DE BOTTON

Alain de Botton was born in Zurich Switzerland December 20, 1969. He studied in Switzerland and then London. De Botton studied history at Cambridge and then completed his Masters Degree in philosophy at Kings College. He is a writer, philosopher, lecturer and documentary producer.

De Botton has published several non-fiction books that examine the relevance of philosophy in our everyday lives.

Some of his non-fiction books include:

Essays In Love (1993),

The Romantic Movement (1994),

Kiss and Tell (1995),

How Proust Can Change Your Life (1997),

The Consolations of Philosophy (2000),

The Art of Travel (2002),

Status Anxiety (2004),

The Architecture of Happiness (2006),

The Pleasure and Sorrows of Work (2009),

Religion for Atheists (2012),

Art as Therapy (2013).

THE TITLE

The title of the text *The Art of Travel* implies that "Art" is a skill, talent or ability that can be virtuosic. Each individual can develop their own unique way of responding to and engaging with the opportunities presented by travel and the landscapes encountered. De Botton proposes that this skill is something that can be trained and developed- as with all skill development – what the reader is exhorted to do is analyse the discrete parts of the travel experience and develop techniques to engage meaningfully with the different interpretation of the landscapes visited.

The art of analysing experience allows travellers to interpret the nuances of the environment around them and understand their own response to it. To support a reader's understanding of the concept, de Botton guides the reader through his own development in the art of travel, as he engages meaningfully with different landscapes and environments. He also relies on the expertise of renowned travellers, writers, artists, poets and explorers.

CONTEXT

De Botton's *The Art of Travel* was originally published in 2002 in a world where the desire to travel had become widespread. The idea of travelling and going on holidays has only established itself in the last two hundred years. Prior to this, only the rich could afford to travel. According to The World Trade Organisation, travel is the world's largest industry.

This text was also originally published in Great Britain where around one in four Brits travel abroad on package holidays. These figures, according to the Office of National Statistics rose closer to one in two in 2013. Globalisation has made travelling more affordable and convenient but it has also changed the purpose of travelling. In the past, the purpose of travel was to educate oneself and make new discoveries but globalization has altered these values and travel has now become a much more commercial experience focusing on the individual as consumer. The rise of terrorism has again impacted the travel industry in recent times.

De Botton asks us to question- What is the point of travel? Why is it that some of our travels impact us greatly and allow us to look at the world from a different perspective? Why do other travel experiences leave us miserable, annoyed and disappointed? De Botton aims to provide his readers with examples of how journeys, no matter how exotic or everyday, can be appreciated. De Botton reminds us of the power of all types of landscapes and the tremendous impact that these landscapes can have on us psychologically and emotionally.

THE PURPOSE OF THE TEXT

By engaging the reader in a conversation about how to understand and identify aspects of the landscape, de Botton is able to show how travelling can inspire us to view our lives differently. This journey, which the reader is invited to join, transforms our understanding of our place in the world around us. The text exhorts us to move from a reliance on the packaged commercialised travel often presented in society, to a greater awareness and reliance on our own ability to interpret real, imagined and remembered landscapes. This ultimately leads to a restored sense of order in our lives, consequently making us happier, healthier and more balanced.

NON FICTION TECHNIQUES

Writers of expository texts use non-fiction techniques. These techniques help to shape meaning and create understanding for the reader. Expository texts are texts whose purpose is to inform or describe.

Structure

The text is delineated into five sections: *Departure, Motives, Landscape, Art* and *Return.* Each section represents a stage in the process of travelling and includes our reasons for travelling and the experiences we have while visiting different cultures and landscapes. Each of these five sections is further broken down into two chapters except the last, which only has one chapter. Within each of these chapters the analysis of the "art" of travel is broken into smaller sub sections or parts, which aim to present points clearly and simply. Each chapter has between 6-9 parts. The reader is initially engaged by the use of opening anecdotes in each chapter. De Botton's colloquial, conversational style and descriptive language help include the reader in a seeming conversation about travel experiences. In so doing, a link to the philosophical analysis of the "skill" of travel is discussed in each chapter.

The table below lists some non-fiction techniques found in *The Art of Travel.* In your responses, be sure to include analysis and the relevance of techniques to the elective, Representing People and Landscapes. Markers do not want shopping lists of techniques, yet techniques are closely linked to representations and this should be recognised.

Descriptive language, figurative language and imagery
Enumeratio and Listing
Sequence of events
Comparison and Contrast
Cause and effect
Problem and Solution
Selection of detail, facts, events (selectivity as to what is included);
Structure of information; format and presentation
Use of persona, point of view;
Use of anecdotes, analogies, allusions, metaphors
Expanding boundaries of factual reporting (exaggeration, embellishing, expanding)
Choice of words and use of language (eg colloquialisms); connotative and emotive language
Use and creation of tone (author's attitude to subject)
Use of dialogue
Use of humour
Use of facts, data, statistics, authority figures
Rhetorical argument and user of rhetorical devices; questions, rhetorical questions;
Narrative techniques- characterization, setting and point of view
Artworks, Photographs
Foregrounding; use of repetition and rephrasing
Capsule biography
Personal Anecdotes
Bon Mots

SECTION AND CHAPTER ANALYSIS

DEPARTURE

Two chapters, *On Anticipation* and *On Travelling Places,* expose our real reason for wanting to travel and the excitement associated with this. De Botton frames the text by identifying our need to escape from the time and place (landscape) we are in now because it is too stressful, busy or cold. We anticipate how our life and relationships will be improved by our engagement with an imagined landscape. The concluding realisation is that the landscapes, while giving us a different perspective on our experiences and relationships, do not actually change the circumstances of our lives.

William Hodges, *Tahiti Revisited*, 1776

I On Anticipation

Structure: Eight parts

Landscapes: Hammersmith London – the author's home and Barbados

Guide: J.-K Huysmans

Images: Three – two paintings and one photograph

Anticipation is associated with hope, eagerness and expectation but in this first chapter de Botton challenges the audience to develop an understanding of the "relationship between the anticipation of travel and its reality". If human beings are motivated by a need to find contentment and happiness, how is this reflected in our travelling? He suggests that rather than thinking deeply about how the different landscapes connect us more meaningfully with ourselves and others, we are controlled by advertising and guide books and are too focused on the where, why and how of travelling. We rarely stop to realise that by moving landscapes we have not inherently changed, but take the same concerns and personalities with us.

This paradox between the real and imagined is shown on the title page of this section. A detailed road map of Hammersmith, London is juxtaposed with an image of the natural openness of sky, palm trees and beach of Barbados. This is then separated by a line under which is a very austere image of J.-K. Huysmans, our guide for this journey between real and imagined worlds. The images represent the detailed prescription of one setting and the openness of the other. The contrasting images suggest disparity and this creates an uneasiness for the responder.

De Botton undermines the excitement of anticipation using the metaphorical representation of Hammersmith's winter as a person descending into "old age". The descriptive listing of aspects of the weather and nature; temperature, "rain", "wind," "leaves", "clouds", "sky", "parks", grass, "mud", firmly place the reader into a landscape descending into winter. The use of biblical imagery when describing the context used in classical art such as "the perfect backdrop to the crucifixion of Christ", connotes the absolute despair and absence of hope experienced in December and the sadness that landscapes can portray. This creates an urgency to escape despair and regain hope by moving into the light.

This dark reality is compared to the memory of the "heat of the previous summer". Providing a landscape that created "a sense of freedom and expansiveness", although foreign, will form the motivation to travel. The use of the colour imagery of "turquoise" and "white", creates a feeling of hope arising from the darkness. Through the use of hyperbolic emotive language "open, free, warm and luxuriant," de Botton has created an ideal, tropical landscape that represents the perfection of a promised land. This idealised world of *Tahiti Revisited,* represented in art, was exhibited at the Royal Academy and provides the reader with an historical precedent for the feelings of happiness in another, imagined landscape.

De Botton's examined anecdote of reading the brochure provides the reader with an understanding of the response to the image of Tahiti, suggesting that this is not new but integral to the human condition. Travelling is an opportunity for escape and renewal, to feel that lightness of spirit and rebirth, away from the reality of an English winter. The use of sensory imagery in the illustrated brochure such as 'barefoot', 'luxuriant' and 'sweet smelling' entices the reader into a setting of overwhelming beauty that reawakens hope and relief from the dreary life of winter in Hammersmith. This brief feeling of elation and free will is subverted by the negative purpose of the advertising in the alliteration of p in "prey" and "power". Yet, because of our longing, hyperbolically described as "touching" and "bathetic" we are willing to be convinced by what an imagined landscape offers. The sensory descriptions persuade readers.

The guide for this chapter is J.–K. Huysmans who recounts the anticipation and expectation of the aristocrat Duc des Esseintes and his motivation to travel. The focus of this novel was the "relationship between the anticipation of travel and its reality." Des Esseintes, pessimistically imagines a landscape and journey. De Botton displays this through the cumulative list of negative images associated with the experience of travel; "run to the station", "fight for a porter", "endure unfamiliar beds", "stand in queues". As a consequence Des Esseintes returned home to spend time reading books rather than physically travelling. His imagined pleasure was not as great as his imagined discomfort, so he resorted to vicarious travel.

De Botton's own experience of traveling to Barbados was also tinged with disappointment. The string of short, factual statements, "The seat cloth is grey.....We look back inside...." identifies the real experience we have travelling rather than the imagined ideal. The simplified, "he journeyed through the afternoon" omits the details of the experience. Even when de Botton finally encounters the "dawn light" and "the sky [that] was pale-blue" from the brochure it is juxtaposed with the reality of his life which consists of a "sore throat", "worry" and "pressure across both temple[s]" (similar to Duc des Esseintes' negative thoughts). His conclusion is that life is multifaceted and that humans are complex.

We travel to attain happiness as it provides us with a sense that there is more to life. This enables the individual to reconnect with themselves through their memories and close connection with a distant landscape. Thus providing a motivation and a justification for travelling.

II On Travelling Places

Structure: Eight parts

Landscapes: The Service Station
The Airport
The Plane
The Train

Guides: Charles Baudelaire, Edward Hopper

Images: Eight – four paintings and four photographs

De Botton explores the powerful impact that 'liminal travelling places' can have on the individual psyche. He suggests that whilst these places may present themselves as 'architecturally miserable' and can often evoke a sense of 'sadness', they may indeed offer a sense of connection, comfort and 'reflection' for those feeling lonely and isolated.

De Botton initially presents the audience with a dual split layout of visual images on the title page for this section. This immediately suggests the physical separation and disconnection of people and places. The stern and formal looking faces of Baudelaire and Hopper, separated by a line from the images of places such as the service station and airport heighten the notion of a gulf existing between the personal and the physical. The visual also suggests that the relationship between people and places may not initially seem an organic or natural process.

De Botton, however, immediately subverts this notion by presenting a personal recount of his journey to a service station. His journey sees him encounter a 'red sky' and 'ornamental trees'. Here, his repeated use of descriptive natural imagery coupled with his observation that he was 'alone with clouds forming on the horizon' creates a very Romantic image–with allusions to Casper David Friedrich's artwork 'Wanderer Above the Sea of Fog'. Consequently this imagery suggests man's unity with nature and the power of the landscape to offer the individual an opportunity for self-reflection and hence, a spiritually transformative experience.

Edward Hopper, Gas, 1940

De Botton then purposefully contrasts this Romantic, natural imagery to the service station. Here, the landscape of the service station is described utilising industrial imagery. Words such as 'illuminated,' 'metal runway,' 'beige putty' and the 'enamel smile of a woman' staring out of a poster create a stark contrast to the beauty of the natural landscape. De Botton describes the building as, 'architecturally miserable', smelling of 'frying oil and lemon scented floor polish'. 'The food [is] glutinous and the tables [are] dotted with islands of dried ketchup from the meals of long departed travellers, and yet something about the scene moved [him].' Here de Botton's use of multisensory imagery and listing aims to disgust the reader. His use of conjunction, however, coupled with emotive language such as 'moved me' and then followed by 'there was an air of reflection, of sadness too...

'surprises the reader and allows them to grapple with the notion that what is often considered an uninspiring landscape can surprisingly provide an individual with reflective and meaningful experiences.

De Botton observes how 'The geographical isolation [of the service station] enforced the atmosphere of solitude in the dining area. The lighting was unforgiving, bringing out pallor and blemishes. The chairs and seats, painted in childishly bright colours had the strained jollity of a fake smile.' Here the repeated use of sentences beginning with the definite article 'the' has the effect of listing and creating a sense of sterility and hollowness through its description of objects. The audience imagines an artificial environment lacking in authenticity and depth of meaning and the effect is to find it repulsive, distancing and uninspiring. However, de Botton cleverly subverts the audience's response by personally reflecting on how such an environment could, in fact, erase extreme feelings of loneliness and generate an understanding in the individual that they are not alone- reminding us of the Romantic's belief in the transformative and spiritual power of nature. De Botton states that his experience of the service station was actually a transformative one, 'I felt lonely, but for once this was a gentle, even pleasant kind of loneliness, rather than unfolding against a backdrop of laughter and fellowship, in which I would suffer from a contrast between my mood and the environment, it had its locus in a place where everyone was a stranger, where the difficulties of communication and the frustrated longing for love seemed to be acknowledged and brutally celebrated by the architecture and the writing.' This very long sentence captures the overwhelming impact that the landscape of the service station had on de Botton. It erased a range of debilitating emotions such as desperate loneliness, suffering and frustration. His repeated use of the conjunction 'where' helps to ease his sense of loneliness by connecting him to others suffering from the same emotional isolation in that landscape. De Botton's self reflection, catalysed by his experience in the service station, provides him with a transformative experience that, paradoxically, allows him to find a small sense of emotional relief and new connection within society.

De Botton concludes that 'it is perhaps to 'lonely service stations that we should drive when there is no one for us to love or hold.' His low modality statement persuades the reader that, paradoxically, landscapes such as lonely service stations can act in a nurturing way, providing respite from feelings of loneliness and isolation.

Charles Baudelaire

De Botton provides the reader with a brief biographical recount of the French poet Charles Baudelaire to further his argument that connection may be found in transitory spaces instead of familiar and stereotypical spaces associated with comfort and belonging. De Botton presents Baudelaire as an outsider utilising emotive language and a list of personal reasons to explain Baudelaire's detachment from his Parisian landscape. 'From an early age he felt uncomfortable at home...In adulthood he could not find a place in bourgeois society...he quarrelled with his mother and stepfather...'. De Botton's utilisation of a factual tone helps to persuade the reader that Baudelaire's fractured relationships and inability to connect with society catalysed his attraction to transient places of travel. Baudelaire's exclamatory observations and repeated use of the imperative serves to emphasise people's need to escape their present oppressive atmosphere and travel. This is seen in his emphatic statements 'Carriage take me with you! Ship, steal me away from here!' as well as his 'Anywhere! Anywhere! So long as it is out of this world.' In using Baudelaire as an example of someone who finds comfort in transitory spaces, de Botton gives credibility to his thesis, that a famous, intelligent, creative being also felt oppressed and stifled by the ordinary world around him.

Trains and Planes

De Botton argues that 'transitory' spaces, landscapes associated with trains and planes can often allow for introspective reflection, stimulate thought as well as provide relief from the pressures of the everyday world. De Botton suggests that it is the 'flow of the landscape' that allows for this movement of thought which may otherwise have been stalled if we were in a different 'static' landscape. He believes that the experience of connecting with a moving landscape is so psychologically and emotionally powerful that, 'At the end of hours of train dreaming we may feel we have been returned to ourselves.'

Like trains, planes also have the ability to provide an individual with a transformative experience. De Botton contrasts light and heavy imagery to show the imaginative freedom that may be gained from one's experience on a plane as opposed to the confining effects of the physical world. For instance the 'eternal mobility' of a plane can offer 'an imaginative counterweight to feelings of stagnation and confinement.' Furthermore de Botton uses the symbol of the plane's ascent to visually portray the imagination's ability to be inspired and create 'decisive shifts in our own lives'. He also uses simile, coupled with parenthetical aside to showcase the fulfilling and enriching experiences an individual may encounter in these transformative spaces, 'Food, that if sampled in a kitchen, would be banal or even offensive, acquires a new taste and interest in the presence of the clouds (like a picnic of bread and cheese that delights us when eaten on a cliff top above a pounding sea). His personal anecdote reinforces how he too has drawn comfort and relief from feelings of sadness by 'the sight of the ceaseless landing and take-off of aircraft'. The insertion of pages which include photographs of clouds (from the perspective of an aircraft passenger) persuades the reader of the comfort and freedom that one can experience in this landscape and aims to convince them that 'It is not necessarily at home we encounter our true selves.'

'Isolated places offer us a material setting for an alternative to the selfish ease, the habits and confinement of the ordinary, rooted world.'(p60)

Edward Hopper

De Botton further reinforces his argument – that one can be inspired by places that aren't often considered inspirational – by making reference to the American artist Edward Hopper's works. By naming specific examples from Hopper's collection, de Botton shows how individuals can be artistically inspired from 'often derided landscapes'. De Botton initially provides a list of Hopper's artworks that have been inspired by what people consider to be ordinary and often mundane landscapes such as hotel rooms, gas stations, diners and trains. De Botton's numerical listing of Hopper's numerous artworks visually implies the extent to which Hopper was inspired by what people considered ordinary and uninspiring landscapes.

De Botton utilises Hopper's artwork *Automat* as an example of how an otherwise unremarkable landscape can inspire an artwork that offers its audience some relief from their own emotional isolation and a connection to others.

He describes the central character of the artwork using emotive language. The central figure of the artwork is a woman sitting at a coffee shop table— looking 'self conscious' and 'afraid'. De Botton imagines her suffering from 'betrayal' or 'loss'. However, he observes that in painting such an isolated and lonely figure, Hopper puts us on the side of the outsider-on the side of those, 'who have failed to find a home in the ordinary world' in a 'world of 'wallpaper and framed photos.' Here, 'a world of wallpaper and framed photos' symbolises a manufactured and artificial landscape. De Botton uses description to represent a landscape of genteel suburban conformity that not every unique individual can relate to nor find acceptance in. De Botton concludes with the paradoxical notion that 'we may dilute a feeling of isolation in a lonely public place and hence rediscover a distinctive sense of community.' The point is made that for some individuals, a relationship with their landscape is imperative to their emotional and psychological well-being. Whether the landscape is physical such as the service station or imaginative, as in Hopper's artworks, it can offer individuals a transformative experience from their current state of being. It can arouse in them a glimmer of hope, relief from their desolate mood, a connection to the greater world and a spiritual refuge, a 'sanctuary' from which to escape the pressures of their own world. While such notions are often associated with nature and the Romantic movement, an interesting subversion occurs here in terms of these iconic urban landscapes and how they can be viewed in a new light. Traditionally such places are viewed negatively and pragmatically. here they are associated with hope and redemption for those who enter and associate with them.

MOTIVES

Amsterdam

The second section, Motives and the chapters, *On the Exotic* and *On Curiosity,* describe travel through the perspective of nature and through questioning what is significant to the individual in causing them to travel. Does the individual wish to see things because they are exotic and thereby suggestive of a sense of excitement because the individual is curious? Both of these reasons are complementary but again de Botton draws the reader in. He enables the reader to analyse each motive carefully in order to develop a greater understanding and empathy for our need and expectation to travel. De Botton presents a chapter that redefines us, our well-being and our intellectual growth.

III On the Exotic

Structure: Eight parts

Landscapes: Amsterdam and Egypt

Guide: Flaubert

Images: Seven – Four paintings/lithographs and three photographs

In the 18th Century, with political stability in Europe and the ability for individuals to travel to develop an understanding of the cultures and art of the east, an interest in the development of the exotic arose. The exotic was seen as something unusual, different, often bizarre but mysterious and outlandish, something to be understood and learnt from. The comparison of Flaubert's perception of the Orient and the exotic, with de Botton's visit to Amsterdam, provides the reader with an examination of the engagement with a culture and landscape different from our own. This allows the opportunity for an individual to redefine who they are through the use of their imagination and their connection to different people, places and races rather than through their place of birth.

De Botton's art of being able to see a difference in the smallest things creates a sense of delight and shows us how to engage meaningfully with the environment around us. The description of the physical characteristics of the "bright yellow" sign in the airport as opposed to its "mundanity" shows his willingness to be excited by the small and different aspects of the environment. Through the repetitive use of "simple" and "simplicity" juxtaposed with the adjective "exotic" de Botton identifies the importance of expectations in shaping our understanding of new places. He explains how the sign is "evidence" that he has arrived somewhere different and that it becomes a "symbol" of being abroad. The cumulative listing of the "plug", "tap", "jam jar", show that observation of the smallest items synecdochially reflects the nationalism of a country. This understanding shown by the repetitive use of difference emphasises the motive for travelling is that it is change and can lead to "the possibility of happiness".

Descriptions of the exotic in Victor Hugo's *Les Orientales* motivated Flaubert. This is shown through his repetition of "I am bored" with France and the French in his diary. This urges him to search for something beyond the trite and meaningless "good civilisation." Egypt and images of "pirates, pashas, sultans, spices, moustaches and dervishes" proved inspirational. This wish to escape the negative connotations of the "peevish pettiness" of his life in Rouen is juxtaposed with the emotive description of the "burning, blue, gold" and the use of declarative statements as in " the Orient!" Reference to "Asiatic women!" emphasises his motivation to escape to a place of greater beauty and freedom. The caesura shows how he is pausing to imagine the difference in the two environments. His lyrical rhyme and alliteration in, " blue seas, a pure sky, silver sands" and the anaphoric use of " Long live the sun , Long live orange trees.." reflects his sense of expected contentment and happiness in Egypt. Flaubert's understanding of the exotic has created a relationship between his happiness and the people and landscape of the Orient.

What de Botton finds exotic in the landscape of Amsterdam is due to his "dissatisfaction with [his] own country". He finds contentment and connection in the landscape of Amsterdam as Flaubert did in Egypt. The comparison of the landscape of Amsterdam and Egypt shows that it is our perception of the elements which motivates us.

The landscape in Amsterdam is ordered and there is an "absence of ostentation". The adjectives describe a "long", "low", "straight", small scene which presents the image of a planner's "...socialist garden city". The urgency of the repetition of "I want" reflects de Botton's deep yearning to find connection and suggests the need for the simplicity suggested. The connotations of the "red front door" emphasise a life different to his, a life of innocent openness and simplicity coupled with the purity of the white walled room with white sheets. The hunger he had "searched for in vain at home" was apparent in the "comfortable" "honest", society that lacked ostentation but was one of "order, cleanliness and light".

Flaubert found Egypt exotic because he felt that bourgeoisie French society suffocated individuality. The derogatory description of the French bourgeois, with their, "Prudery, snobbery, smugness, racism and pomposity" reflects Flaubert's belief in the restrictive mindset of the French middle classes. Flaubert compared them to "sheep" and believed that they were so disconnected from the meaning and simplicity of life that they could be controlled and moved by others. The satirical list in "A Suspicion of Artistic Endeavour" reflects his antipathy to the attitudes and beliefs of French society. He exposes the banality of their lives and how they are devoid of sincere and deep relationships with those around them. The use of clichés and stereotypes in "In tolerance and ignorance..." minimalises the reader's understanding of others.

Flaubert's hyperbolic description of the French reflects his unwillingness to engage with the nuances of society. He creates a caricature of the French people. The use of listing in this passage gives the impression that this is a serious and scientific analysis rather than a personal opinion.

Bazaar of the Silk Mercers, Cairo, lithograph by Louis Haghe after a drawing by David Roberts

The insincerity of his perception of the French parallels de Botton's relationship with England. Both are searching for a greater connection with the elements of life through the metaphor of a different country. The luxury of the "exotic" is symbolised through the use of colours "purple, gold, and turquoise". This inclusion of the quote from an English traveller (Edward Lane) adds authority to the belief in the beauty of the chaotic, baroque life, in a landscape that is not controlled by the mannered French bourgeoisie.

Memory and imagination can also shape our relationship with landscapes, affecting what we remember, what we forget and what we idolise. The inventing of stories to create a memory or an image behind the individual- the image of the Eugene Delacroix's painting *Women of Algiers in Their Apartment* (1835) creates the desire to develop a relationship with people in their own environment. Both de Botton and Flaubert identify a woman with whom they develop a real or imaginary relationship. The use of the personal pronouns, "I", "me", and "myself" reflects the self-centred relationship that has developed between the individual and the image that is represented by a different culture. This motivates the traveller to value what is "missing from [their] own culture". The travellers then link themselves to the environment.

The images in this section of the text reflect the overwhelming impact of the landscape on individuals and the subjectivity implicit in its interpretation. The height and use of shadow and perspective in the image *"Bazaar of the Silk Mercers, Cairo,"* a lithograph by Haghe after a drawing by David Roberts, reflects the unknown, as the eye of the viewer is drawn around the corner and into the shadows of the distance. As with the image, *Street in Amsterdam* and Lane's *Private Houses in Cairo* the eye is drawn down and beyond the image. The reader is connected to the curiosity of the landscape, what is beyond and is almost invited by the artist into the exotic and our own memories and imagination.

The significance of Amsterdam and the Egyptian landscape offers the travellers an opportunity to see life differently, to find what they have been searching for in their own countries but have not been able to see or find. This allows individuals to form connections with societies that reflect this understanding of human existence rather than national allegiance. They are able to understand human existence through another "history and mindset" which has the power to transform their understanding of others and themselves within the world.

IV On Curiosity

Structure: Ten parts

Landscapes: Madrid

Guide: Alexander von Humboldt

Images: Five – three paintings, one photograph and one map

De Botton constructs a chapter that utilises contrast and juxtaposition between himself and the German explorer, naturalist and geographer Humboldt to show the differing effects of landscape on individuals. Primarily, de Botton is saddened by the modern commercialised travel experience where everything has been factually outlined in tourist guidebooks. He bemoans the value of each monument having been judged and awarded a number of stars and guide-books which tell travellers how they should feel when experiencing the landscape. De Botton finds this challenging and seriously damaging to our curiosity and ultimately to our emotional and psychological well-being. His response emphasises the importance of curiosity and discovery. We should take something new from landscapes and their ability to impact our sense of well-being as well as our intellectual growth and wonder should not be compromised.

De Botton's response to the landscape

De Botton feels dull and uninspired even though he has the chance to explore Madrid. On his hotel room desk lie

> *'several magazines offered by the hotel with information on the city and two guidebooks that I had brought from home. In their different ways, they conspired to suggest that an exciting and multifarious phenomenon called Madrid was waiting to be discovered outside. Maps of monuments, churches, museums, fountains, plazas and shopping streets.'*

His listing here implies the overwhelming bombardment of information created by the advertising medium as well as advertising's forceful ability to tell you what you must do. His reaction to this is one of 'listlessness and self-disgust.' He physically retreats to escape the 'noise' and prefers 'to remain in bed and, if possible, catch an early flight home'. This suggests that one's landscape and the pressure to explore it, can be debilitating to the psyche.

When de Botton eventually ventures out into the landscape of Madrid and finds himself on the corner of Calle De Carretas and the Puerta del Sol looking at the monument of Carlos III he wonders with mounting anxiety, what [he] was to do here, what [he] was to think'. The fragmentation caused by the punctuation shows how de Botton has been rendered passive and inarticulate both linguistically and intellectually by the amount of factual information bombarding him. He feels he has been robbed of his curiosity and wonder. This can be seen in the repetition of the pronoun 'everything' when he frustratingly states that 'in Madrid everything was already known, everything had already been measured.' De Botton laments his own loss of curiosity arousing experiences and soothes his wounds by reflecting on Humboldt's experiences 'it was fortunate for him that almost every exciting fact about South America was wrong and questionable,' and that 'Humboldt did not suffer such intimidation.' Instead de Botton is left following The Michelin Street Guide to Madrid which points its needle 'resolutely, towards, among other targets, a brown looking staircase in the echoing corridors of the Monasterio de las Dascalzas Reale'. This acts as a final symbol of the oppressive control that travel guide books have over our intellect and senses. The needle is 'resolute' offering its reader a painful 'no way out', whilst the muted and dull 'brown' colouring of the staircase suggests the lack of excitement that is to follow in his journey to the Monasterio. The staircase can also be symbolic of a path leading to nowhere, suggesting that de Botton feels his journey will be pointless and lack meaning. De Botton thus asks his readers for sympathy. He feels that when a landscape does not inspire curiosity in the individual then they should be allowed to 'remain in bed and take the next flight home.'

Eduard Ender, *Alexander von Humboldt and Aimé Bonpland in Venezuela*, c. 1850

Humboldt's response to the landscape

De Botton contrasts his experiences with an account of the then twenty nine year old German, Humboldt. The passages detailing Humboldt's travels and discoveries are written in a faster pace and are energetic, conjuring images of curiosity, wonder, delight and passion to discover new possibilities. De Botton lists Humboldt's achievements and discoveries. These serve to provide the audience with a wide variety of Humboldt's achievements such as 'He redrew the map of South America...he was the first to discover that magnetic intensity declines the further one is from poles...[he gave the] first account of the rubber and cinchona trees,' and recreates the energy and enthusiasm which drove him. Humboldt is presented by de Botton as an individual who is challenged and stimulated by his landscape. The landscape inspires Humboldt's drive, ambition and his curiosity. De Botton substantiates this with a direct quote from Humboldt, where he outlines how the study of maps and travel books 'aroused in me a secret fascination that was at times almost irresistible.' To reinforce Humboldt's credibility de Botton quotes renowned essayist, poet and lecturer, Ralph Waldo Emerson's observations acknowledging Humboldt as a man, 'who wanted to show the possibilities of the human mind.'

De Botton peppers the description of the landscapes that Humboldt experiences with luscious visual imagery, enticing the reader and capturing their imagination with an unspoilt terrain. Details such as 'The hills of calcareous rock on which the town stood were dotted with cacti and opuntia, their trunks branching out like candelabras coated with lichen,' are beautifully crafted, utilising similes to create an exotic, yet elegant atmosphere, where the physical creations of man have a symbiotic relationship with nature. In this landscape, man and nature have again become one. De Botton highlights the perfection and unity of man and nature when curiosity allows an individual to be led to new discoveries.

He also creates a sense of danger, excitement and adventure when detailing Humboldt's expeditions. For instance he directly quotes Humboldt's account of one of his expeditions to show the joy and thrill that can be obtained when experiencing a landscape for the first time. Humboldt recounts 'we were constantly climbing through clouds...the ridge was not wider than eight or ten inches...On the right lay a fearful abyss.' Here, the use of emotive language coupled with the descriptive visual imagery depicts an atmosphere of imaginative wonder and stimulating fear created by Humboldt's experience of a foreign landscape. The statistical description of the size of the ridge also creates a threatening and challenging atmosphere. De Botton feels robbed of such experience in his 21st century environment where travellers research before embarking on journeys and fresh discoveries are minimised.

LANDSCAPE

In this section the two chapters, *On the Country and the City* and *On the Sublime,* discuss the impact a landscape and its beauty can have on our ability to deal with aspects of modern life. Wordsworth's concept of "spots of time" is explored in relation to the impact that the natural landscape can have on an individual's well-being. The Romantic concept of the sublime beauty of landscape is also explored. Whether real or remembered, it has the power to transform us to another place and emotional state as it allows us to remove ourselves, however briefly from the clutter and chaos of everyday life and come back refreshed and restored. This is the "art" of travel.

Sparrow's Nest,"Look, five blue eggs are gleaming there!..."(p135)

V On the Country and the City

Structure: Seven parts

Landscape: The Lake District

Guide: William Wordsworth

Images: Three – Two paintings and one photograph

The development of the "city" in the 1800s as a result of the Industrial Revolution not only created an affluent and educated middle class but it also created the travel industry. The development of an extensive train network provided the opportunity for people to travel to the country. The Romantic poet Wordsworth, who eventually became England's Poet Laureate, developed the concept of the beauty of nature being able to restore and transform individuals who had been corrupted by the life of the city.

The idea that there was dichotomy between the country and the city was new in the 1800s. Before this time England was a largely agrarian society, but with the development of industry, people had the time and opportunity to move freely between one and the other. De Botton is ironically using the same mode of transport as the 1800s traveller to escape the city for the restorative landscape of the country. The juxtaposition of the "mechanical sound" of the microwave compared to the country "cows" shows a gentler more relaxed feeling which leads to the "uninhibited yawn". This reflects the changes that occur upon moving away from the city. This is continued with the comparison of the autumnal colour of the homely "large" car to the pristine industrialised "vacuum cleaner" which reflects the differences between the two landscapes. The statistical evidence to support a reader's understanding of the changes in lifestyle reflects how the mechanised world needs to label items and record the size and quantity of events. The imagery of the small village, only a "few miles", "narrow beds" and the lack of specific detail regarding size, belies the number of people who had visited in the 1800s. This again creates a divide between the country and the city. The natural imagery of the view from the window in the hotel and symbolism of the wise owl reflects the restful and restorative nature of the country environment.

Wordsworth was a Romantic poet and although initially seen as strange, he eventually became the Poet Laureate, transforming the way that English people related to the landscape. M, de Botton's companion, although commenting that Wordsworth was "an old toad" was able to quote lines of his poetry from memory. Her recitation of Wordworth's 'Ode: Intimations of Immortality. X' creates an image of the peacefulness created by nature while the compound word "fit-full" shows the difficulty that city dwellers have with reconciling the peace of nature to new landscapes. The description of Wordsworth beginning with the negative preposition "despite", to explain that he was physically not "well-made", contrasts with his ability to effectively relate with the minute detail of the landscape such as that seen in his observations of the "butterfly", "cuckoo", "daisy" and "small celandine". The section of his poetry quoted has a simple aabbccdd rhyming scheme—almost doggerel in style, but the detail creates a sense of pleasure and joy in the simplicity of natural life.

This again presents a central theme in de Botton's text, that simplicity and a lack of complication in our lives gives us pleasure. This is the philosophy of nature expounded by Wordsworth, "that Nature was necessary to repair the damage of the psychological and physical damage life in the city". It is labelled Romanticism by somed. This concept was not initially well accepted and was considered to be negatively "forced, strained and unnatural". The archaic adjective "stoic" clearly describes Wordsworth's belief and defence of the importance of nature to the well-being of individuals.

Wordsworth believed that the City was corrupting to the soul. It was associated with the seven deadly sins including pride. The city environment thrived on competition and fed anxiety. The desire for the new did not bring happiness. In actual fact, neighbours knew little of each other and this meant that nature did not have redemptive powers as there was no connection between the people in the city. The harsh and unfeeling "decadent orange florescent glow" reflected on the cloud, making it appear granite grey. The transient elements of the city (fluorescent) clashed against the rock (granite) of nature. De Botton takes a photograph of a cloud that follows the industrial path to the sea. The movement away from the city creates a sense of peace for de Botton. This leads him to remember the imagined landscape created by Wordsworth's most acclaimed poem 'Lines written a few miles above Tintern Abbey'. Even the title suggests that unformed nature and fluidity with no precise distance or time creates a sense of openness and calm.

To further engage the reader in an understanding of the overwhelming power of the natural landscape de Botton uses the rhetorical question "Why?' to engage in the context of the Lakes District and take us on his own transformative journey. The emotive description of the "luxuriant" valley is juxtaposed with the formulaic and uninspiring *Mortal Man* breakfast room. Even the news is now a murmur whereas earlier it made noise and had to be turned off. Now the power of the landscape has so enthralled that they no longer hear the news. The adjectives describing size and distance are not precise. For example "little" and "great" are the size of the town and they travel into the "deep countryside" reflecting the unrestricted nature of the landscape.

Here they encounter an oak which is personified as "noble", an archetypal symbol of age, maturity, longevity and strength. The lyrical description of the oak, its size, shape and comfort, even its shadow, is sheltering, solid and majestic. The pathetic fallacy of rain, symbolic of the cleansing of the forest and the individual and the onomatopoeic "pitter-patter" creates a harmonious setting in nature. We are continually drawn into the remembered world of Wordsworth through the use of poetry. The Lakes District becomes a metaphor for gaining renewal both physically and emotionally, creating a deep sense of calm as reflected in "sending fingers deep in the clammy soil".

The individual's search for understanding and peace within his or her life was the prompt for Wordsworth to develop his theories of nature. He accepted that individual personalities were "malleable" and that we can be transformed by a closeness to nature. Alliteration of "conscious concerns" emphasises that the inanimate do not actively judge or persuade us, therefore this willingness to find peace and balance must be within each of us. The trees are used to symbolise the values of the country, "oaks dignity, pines resolution, lakes calm". Wordsworth, and by implication de Botton, suggest that human happiness and contentment can be found in nature because of its "sanity ,purity and permanence ". Note the rhyme of "ity" and the alliteration of "p" which reflects the complex relationship between all three nouns and by intimation between the reader and the landscape. The symbolism of flowers personify the Christian characteristics of humility and meekness while animals are archaically "stoic." Such descriptions Wordsworth referred to earlier in the chapter.

The balance represented by nature and its gentleness is revealed through the onomatopoeic bird calls and the birds' personified pensiveness. The verbs describe the slow pace of the scene as if nature is allowing the reader time to settle. A "caterpillar is walking strenuously", "Sheep amble" and this is heightened by the adjective "lazy mouthful" when describing how the cow chews. The use of the personal pronouns in the question "Why am I me and she she?" allows the reader to contemplate their place in the world. This pastoral ideal is continued by the internal rhyme of "deep green ...Stream". Wordsworth believed that nature had the power to transform individuals and encouraged them "to locate good in themselves"(p151)

Bridge at Brothers Water

De Botton reflects on his short visit to the Lake District and is concerned that the reality will be different to the imagined power of nature. He is surprised to find that nature indeed has the power to impact our daily lives in the city. He recounts his own experience being surrounded by the chaos of the city "oppressed by cares". The remembered landscape allows him a "spot of time" to "protect [himself] against the eddies of anxiety".

De Botton's analysis of the dichotomy of the country and the city, created by the rise of industry, articulates opportunities presented to travellers to appreciate and see the natural landscape and the power it can have over an individual's well-being. The concept of "spots of time" can provide us with a release from the chaos of the city and restore balance to our lives. The country has the power to restore and transform us. The "art" of travel is to understand that a personal connection with nature can provide memories that will create sanity, purity and permanence in the chaos of city life.

VI On the Sublime

Structure: Eight parts

Landscapes: Sinai desert

Guides: Edmund Burke, Job

Images: Six – Three paintings and three photographs

In this chapter de Botton explores the landscape's ability to 'arouse the mind to sublimity.' Dictionary.reference.com defines sublimity as the 'state or quality of being sublime', whilst the word 'sublime' is defined as impressing the mind with a sense of grandeur or power; inspiring awe'. De Botton suggests that 'sublime' landscapes, such as those that are vast, have the ability to impact us both psychologically and emotionally. They can help us to understand and accept our place in this world, as well as offer us relief from the trivial day to day stresses which we allow to overwhelm us. 'Sublime' landscapes can also inspire us to expand our often limited perspective of ourselves and the world around us and can enable us to think beyond ourselves.

In order to experience such revelational feelings de Botton intentionally 'set[s] out for the [Sinai] desert in order to be made to feel small.' De Botton utilises visual imagery of nature's strength and endurance to describe the valley as being '...empty [with]...boulders...strewn across a sandstone floor, as though the stamping of a petulant giant had caused them to roll off the sides.' Here the simile of a giant helps the audience to imagine the vast expanse of the desert as well as its powerful geological construction. Only a mythological creature such as giant could physically make changes to such a substantial and immovable terrain. The giant's power is further reinforced through the plosives used in 'stampede' and petulant'. In contrasting a giant to himself, de Botton also suggests humanity's weakness and impotence when pitted against the forces of nature. Thus, de Botton's word choices and imagery all work to represent the relationships between people and their environments.

Caspar David Friedrich, *Chalk Cliffs in Rügen*, c. 1818

De Botton asks the reader to consider 'What do barren, overwhelming spaces bring us?' The connotations of the double adjective of 'barren', and 'overwhelming' imply that nothing purposeful or fruitful can be gained from experiencing such landscape -only emptiness and exhaustion. However, de Botton then cleverly extolls the virtues of such an empty and vast landscape. He sees earth's ability to withstand the powerful forces of nature throughout history as inspiring. De Botton admiringly observes that, 'There are gashes and fissures that speak of the pressures of millennia...' and that 'The earth's tectonic plates have rippled granite as though it were linen.' Both these sentences function to assert de Botton's awe at the earth's lasting presence as opposed to our temporal one. The 'sh' sound repeated in the first phrase creates disturbing images of the wounds that the earth has elegantly suffered yet survived over time, whilst the simile in the second phrase reinforces the earth's powerful and unpredictable ability to shift and create change in its landscape.

De Botton then focuses closely on the word 'sublime' and its importance in capturing a range emotions and experiences. He initially observes that 'there are few emotions about places for which adequate single words exist; we have to make awkward piles of words to convey what we felt when watching light fade...'. Human language cannot often adequately capture the emotion experienced in such a landscape and the noun 'piles' connotes our linguistic inability and futility to do so. However, de Botton feels that the word 'sublime' can convey the power of landscape to move us. He lists a number of essays as examples where the authors explore the emotional power of landscapes and their ability to evoke '...power, power greater than that of humans and threatening to them.'

Such essays include: Hildebrand's *How the Mind is Raised by the Sublime* and Burke's *A Philosophical Enquiry into the Origin of our Ideas of the Sublime and Beautiful.* These factual works written during the Romantic period help to reiterate de Botton's point of view and give credibility and plausibility to his belief. The Romantics believed that individuals had the propensity to have transformative experiences and gain insight about themselves when interacting with sublime landscapes. Boundless landscapes were defined as sublime during the Romantic period.

Botton provides the reader with images of these landscapes by inserting double and single pages of artwork and photographs into his text. He uses Loutherbourg's *An Avalanche in the Alps* which depicts the threatening and destructive power of nature and its magnitude in comparison to man's small stature, his powerlessness and fear. This is vividly conveyed through the size and positioning of the characters and nature in the artwork. Nature takes up the full frame, whereas man is seen in the far left corner on the bottom quarter of the picture. The comparatively small size of the humans suggests their insignificance and mortal weakness. Some are seen desperately pleading with nature while another attempts to flee the scene. Their faces display both terror and awe—the exact feelings that de Botton asserts are experienced when one encounters 'sublime' landscapes.

The artwork of Caspar David Freidrich, *Chalk Cliffs in Rügen* is also integrated into the text. Again the characters here are depicted as small and featured in the foreground whilst nature takes up the rest of the frame. Nature is indeed the subject of the frame and the subjects once again look on in awe and wonder at its vastness and beauty. De Botton also includes his own photographs of the desert landscape. Throughout the chapter the camera moves from a bird's eye shot, to a wide shot to a full shot of the desert terrain. This inward movement of the shot helps to bring the reader closer and closer to de Botton's own experience encouraging responders to feel the emotions of awe and wonder associated with the landscape. It also metaphorically acts as a visual reminder of how our affinity with a 'sublime' landscape can develop so that we can appreciate its beauty and natural wonder.

De Botton also discusses how our interaction with sublime landscapes can lead to a spiritual awareness and realisation that there must be a higher power greater than all of us. He quotes directly an extract from the Old Testament Book of Job. God's repetitive questioning of Job is intended to showcase Job's ignorance of the mysteries of creation. His powerful and accusatory tone in pointing out Job's absence from creation is intended to make Job realise that 'the universe is greater than [him].' In doing so, he highlights to Job, and consequently to humanity, that there are more powerful mysteries at work and that we shouldn't be upset when things do not work out according to our expectations.

De Botton outlines the emotional and psychological benefits of interacting with a boundless landscape. His use of adjectives increases towards the end of the chapter to reveal how our relationship with a 'sublime' landscape may reveal that we are 'frail', 'insignificant' and 'temporary'. However, de Botton notes this is a good revelation as it conversely allows us to 'accept our limitations' without 'bitterness or lamentation', 'bow to necessities greater than ourselves,' and come away 'inspired by what lies beyond us.'

ART

This fourth section is again broken into two chapters. One *On Eye Opening Art* and the second *On Possessing Beauty*. Both chapters deal with what we retain from our travels, what we go to see and what we feel we need to remember. This section focuses on how we transform experiences into memories and representations. We compare the images created by others before we travel and then reflect on how to interpret and represent these experiences.

VII On Eye-opening Art

Structure: Seven parts

Landscape: Provence

Guide: Vincent van Gogh

Images: Eleven – Five paintings of Provence, Cypress trees and wheat and six photographs of the similar sites currently.

Our interaction with landscapes can be structured by works of art, which both inspire us to visit places and also prescribe the way we relate to them. De Botton, in this chapter, implies that trying to find the expected beauty in a landscape can be difficult and can leave us feeling disappointed. Vincent Van Gogh is the guide for the journey through Provence and his experience articulates the process he undertook to challenge the expectation and the rigid interpretation of the landscape he had inherited. The business of travel can overwhelm our appreciation of the aesthetic as we spend time looking for what we cannot see. We are challenged to engage with the process of the experience rather than the expectation of tourist brochures.

The sceptical expectation de Botton experiences on first visiting Provence is realised in the tone of the opening section. The repetition of "Provence" connotes the beauty of the landscape but there is another reality, beyond the expected refined and aesthetical pleasing scene. The much acclaimed beauty is juxtaposed with the industrial landscape. De Botton becomes confused and rather than seeing the expected beauty is overwhelmed by the "*giant* oil refinery", "*tangled* pipes", and "cooling towers" emphasising his disconnection with the landscape. His reaction reflects the "complexity of the manufacture of liquid in car" rather than the simplistic beauty he was expecting to see. The metaphor of a predator looking for food is shown through the image of the traveller scanning the landscape hedonistically "looking for beauty" with the self-indulgent expectation of being pleased.

Despite the idyllic language which creates an image of a pastoral ideal of quiet, blue cloudless sky, cicadas, cypress trees and distant mountains, de Botton is not impressed by the landscape.

It has failed to live up to the expectation of the memories of others. His discomfort with his inability to see the beauty that exists is shown through the use of negative adjectives; "bored" "uncomfortable" "hot plastic". Yet his personal scepticism of the landscape's purported beauty doesn't restrain him from the recourse to trite clichés of "simply paradise" when meeting his hosts.

Individuals are not as malleable as expected. De Botton's personified eyes are "bewildered at their freedom" because we are organised on holidays and travel to see what is expected and not allowed time to just look. The agitation he feels is shown in the metaphor of a hand drawing a pencil over a map that hasn't any order and seeing unique random patterns. This foreshadows the experience of the impressionist Van Gogh who is renowned for his reinterpretation of light in nature. The colours he saw in a landscape were the bright blue and yellow which developed into a pattern that was not easily discernible or appreciated by his contemporaries. The adverb "Yet" draws the reader into the text and gives an alternative suggestion that aesthetic taste may be less rigid or formulaic. This shows that individuals have the ability to choose and construct their own response to a landscape based on their own expectations and experiences. The sarcastic tone in "the pathos of this fragile and yet essential crop" prompts the reader to question the prescribed explanation of the landscape and rely on their own interpretations.

Art creates a reason for travelling but it also constrains the way we see and react to landscapes. The use of conjunctions such as "because", "yet" and "and", to begin each paragraph, reflect how uncomfortable we feel by being forced into discordant interpretations of nature which have been imposed upon us.

The continued witty metaphor of data in a computer reflects the scepticism that we can be shown how to draw out an understanding from a mass of data. The use of the authoritative, biographical detail of Van Gogh, parallels de Botton's initial journey and experience of travelling to Provence between "olive trees" and the "train station". The preposition "despite" shows that he saw the landscape differently. The cyclical language of the seasons, "snow", "spring", "summer" is a motif that is used through the text and implies that time is necessary to develop an understanding of a landscape.

The complexity of understanding a landscape is shown through Van Gogh's urgent repetition of "quickly..." and the exclamatory language "thirty-five years old!" De Botton presents the concept that experts, such as Van Gogh, acknowledge the importance of self-education learnt from travel. The motif of the "explorer" enables both Van Gogh and de Botton to reassess their surroundings and develop their own interpretations of the landscape around them. Travellers see ideas reframed but question what is accurate and real and doubt their own ability to judge personal impressions and emotions in a new landscape.

Travel, as a business, constructs our understanding of the landscape in order to sell experiences. The perfunctory purpose of the tourist office is reflected in the mundane asyndeton of services offered from "free maps" to "baby-sitting" to "ruins". The guided tour shows that landscapes need to be interpreted for us by a passionate authority in the form of "Sophie" who was "writing a thesis on Van Gogh at the Sorbonne in Paris". Yet, the later alliterative description of the guide as "sadly Sophie" implies the scepticism of not being able to see the building that history had erased, despite photocopied proof of the building.

This means that we need to develop our own background of facts rather than be convinced by the interpretations of others. The imagined and remembered is not the reality and maybe it is the reality that we need to engage with to develop our own relationship with the landscape. The negative, sceptical tone of de Botton is continued in the juxtaposition of the bright colours of the remembered building and the current "student hostel" that was "dwarfed by a giant Monoprix supermarket". The "dissent" in the group underlies his scepticism and can be seen in the use of colloquial language such as, "Well it doesn't look like much". While we may not see the landscape as Van Gogh did, it may be possible to disregard what he saw because he was, at times, mentally unwell. The connotation of the "asylum" is that Van Gogh feared that he would not be understood. Van Gogh's own ambivalence "This really looks too strange" allows the viewer to also acknowledge that we too don't know and perceptions are subjective.

Furthermore, the exaggerated description of the "walls that were crooked", "the sun an unusual colour" and "grass not always green" reinforces the reader's understanding that individual interpretations of landscapes are idiosyncratic. Individual relationships with a landscape are difficult to prescribe and need to be related to personal experiences to be authentic.

De Botton questions whether what is packaged by advertisers as beautiful, is seen that way by all. Artists bring out "valuable feature(s)" of a landscape and this teaches the traveller what to identify. The individual needs to take from the canvas but also transfer places and images to their own world, values and experiences. Photography fulfils the same role, as does the description of the Lake District in England. Despite the negative language used to describe the landscape as "rough", "wild", "hopeless", "sterility", "barren" and "frightful" the painting of these regions, through image and word, develops a travel industry that is still prevalent today. That "we tend to seek out corners of the world only once they have been painted and written about by artist" shows the power of the image in creating or reinforcing a relationship between man and the landscape. Yet, de Botton remains sceptical. Although art can create interest and motive for the reader to travel it cannot create enthusiasm. Travellers need to combine their own understanding with what they are shown to develop their own relationship with the landscape.

Vincent van Gogh, *The Yellow House,* Arles,1888

VIII On Possessing Beauty

Structure: Nine parts

Landscapes: The Lakes District
Madrid
Amsterdam
Barbados
London Dockland

Guide: John Ruskin

Images: Five – One sketch, one diagram, two paintings, one engraving

In this chapter de Botton describes how we as humans endeavour to 'possess' the beauty of a landscape in order to capture and hold onto the 'values' and 'mood' that the landscape impresses upon our emotions and psychology. This serves to highlight the importance of landscapes to individuals and the positive impact that they can have on our emotional and psychological well-being. A human's innate desire to commodify and hence control the experience suggests our inability to effectively retain the memory and feelings associated with a beautiful landscape. Our innate need to own the experience in a quantifiable form emphasises the necessity of experiencing beautiful landscapes in our everyday lives so that our lives are more fulfilling and meaningful.

To begin with, de Botton aims to show the reader that different kinds of landscapes can impact an individual in several ways. He uses personal anecdote to engage the reader and persuade them of the power of different types of landscapes on our psyche. De Botton displays the 'overwhelming' effects of settings on our emotions when he outlines in the opening of the chapter the effect a brick wall in Amsterdam had on him. He uses vivid visual, aural and tactile imagery when describing how he 'took

[his] hands from [his] pockets and ran them along the bricks' gnarled and pitted surface.' The harsh sounding plosives create a distinct and intricate image and texture in the mind of the reader that emphasises the unusual beauty of the bricks. De Botton's reaction to this beauty – an '... impulse to kiss [the bricks], to feel more closely a texture that reminded me of blocks of pumice or halva from a Lebanese delicatessen.'

Again, de Botton utilises tactile imagery. He also introduces gustatory imagery with the halva as one experience triggers the memory of another. The beauty of the landscape here provides him with a multisensory experience that arouses joy and fulfilment.

He is also deeply moved by the view he can see from his window when visiting the Lakes District. It is rather clever coincidence that he is staying at the Mortal Man Inn, a timely reminder of his own temporality and insignificance in contrast to the timeless power of nature. De Botton describes the view from his window. He sees 'hills of soft Silurian rock covered in fine green grass above which a layer of mist was hovering. The hills undulated as though they formed a part of the backbone of a giant beast that had laid down to sleep and might at any point awake...'. The description, which is heavily peppered with adjectives has the effect of creating awe, wonder and an excitable sense of hidden danger in de Botton. This is seen through his use of geological imagery 'Silurian rock' to emphasise to the audience the timeless, pre-historic power of the earth, whilst the simile of a giant beast creates an image of something mysterious, mythical and threatening.

De Botton outlines how we use many 'lower forms' to capture this beauty such as photography, buying souvenirs and carving our name into pillars. His tone is disdainful and critical of man's superficial tendencies as seen through his use of derogatory language such as 'cretin' and 'imbecile' to describe those who damage landscapes in a desperate need to leave an imprint of themselves. He also outlines why individuals feel the need to quantify their experience, 'there is an urge to say, "I was here, I saw this and it mattered to me." There is close resemblance of this tricolonic phrase to Julius Caesar's 'I came, I saw, I conquered'. The allusion, coupled with the parataxis, emphasises the swiftness and immediacy in which individuals wish to capture their experiences and emotions. The anaphora of 'I' reinforces our personal need and possibly harbours a critical undertone towards our selfish desires to immediately capture the experience and then display its impact to others. Both the parataxis and anaphora hint at humanity's ignorance of the landscape that they desire to capture.

De Botton could possibly be criticizing our willingness to commodify the experience without actually taking the time to understand it and appreciate it. Our need for instant gratification renders us ignorant and unappreciative of the wonders in the landscape that lies before us. De Botton thus wants us to spend time understanding the landscape as he feels there are many positive gains that can be made for the individual if they do so. De Botton suggests to the audience that a more meaningful and more intellectual way of possessing a beautiful landscape is through '*understanding* it.' Here he utilises italics to emphasise the delicate nature, depth and complexity of understanding the beauty of a landscape. He believes that a conscious understanding of beautiful landscapes can take place through art, writing or drawing, 'irrespective of whether we happen to have any talent for doing so.' In this way, 'Representing people and landscapes' occur through the process of creating, composing, responding and remembering.

John Ruskin

To support his argument, de Botton introduces the theories of English author and art critic John Ruskin. De Botton uses simple language to explain Ruskin's theories to the audience. Ruskin believed that drawings could 'teach us to see- that is, to notice rather than merely look. In the process of re-creating with our own hands what lies before our eyes, we seem naturally to move from observing beauty in a loose way to one where we acquire a deep understanding of its constituent parts and hence more secure memories of it.'

De Botton also includes direct quotes from Ruskin who believed that 'My efforts are directed not to making a carpenter an artist, but to making him happier as a carpenter.' Here, de Botton supports his argument in that everyone has something to gain from drawing a landscape. Ruskin suggests that one's life will be enriched and made more favourable if they undertake the process of drawing the beauty of the landscape. Drawing a landscape allows us to consider the details that contribute to the beauty of the landscape and hence make it more memorable. De Botton shows this deconstruction of the landscape through his repetitive use of questions when imagining looking at a woodland, 'How do the stems connect to the roots? Where is the mist coming from? Why does one tree seem darker than another?'

John Ruskin, *Study of a Peacock's Breast Feather*, 1873

Finally de Botton utilises a range of nouns, verbs and adjectives to exemplify the myriad of emotions that we may experience when trying to word-paint our encounter with a beautiful landscape. These emotions are often highlighted in italics to show the important effect that they can have on our psyche. A beautiful landscape may enable us to 'make sense of pain', elicit 'nostalgia', 'stir' emotions in us such as 'admiration', 'fright', and 'enchanted pride'. It may make us feel 'strange' *'expansive' 'timid', 'fragile' 'weak'* or even *'comfortless'*.

RETURN

This is the concluding section where de Botton ties the concepts discussed through the text together. There is a juxtaposition and implicit judgement that to fully understand and interact with a landscape and gain emotional restoration we do not need to travel beyond our local area but rather, be more mindful of the way we view and interact with individuals, and the environment in order to develop our own "art of travel".

IX On Habit

Structure: Six parts

Landscape: Hammersmith, London

Guide: Xavier de Maistre

Images: One – De Botton's bedroom

In the last chapter of the text de Botton relates the disillusionment on returning home. The reader is encouraged to look more closely at what exists in their local landscape, at the events of the everyday and to think about what really makes us happy. Readers are urged to decide whether it is the travel or the "art" of attending to the details in the landscape around us that creates a sense of happiness and contentment. Readers are encouraged to question relationships with landscapes and their impact on the development of an internal rather than an external calmness and contentment with the world.

The unhappiness and discomfort that is felt on returning home is obvious from the description of de Botton's emotional state. The repetitive use of past tense "I had... seen, slept, swum" in the opening section compared to the second half of the paragraph where the negative emotions of "I felt... despair, few worse, fated..." emphasise how de Botton felt drained of happiness on returning home. He felt constrained and trapped by the regular landscape and the only happiness was in the remembered one of Barbados. This image of despair and the mundane is further compounded by the use of metaphors as seen in the despondent image, the "park was a pond and the skies funereal". The personified world is "indifferent" to his pain and has no regard for his unhappiness. This realistic depiction of the sadness experienced by many travellers at the end of their journey engages the reader in the conversation to find a way to maintain the emotional high of the travel experience when engaging with everyday landscapes.

Having established a sense of unhappiness, de Botton then refutes this sense of hopelessness with the use of an expert opinion by Pascal, that the problem is not with the landscape or world but within the reader. This epiphany is the only section throughout the text which has one sentence,

" the sole cause of man's unhappiness is that he doesn't know how to stay quietly at home"

It leads the reader to be open to view experiences from a different perspective. The juxtaposition of the intrepid explorer Humboldt, to romantic bedroom traveller De Maistre, appears ludicrous but highlights the similarity in the experience. This comparison is compounded by the asyndeton of Humboldt's travel requirements juxtaposed with De Maistre's simple requirements in the alliterative "pink pyjamas". Yet the justification of the similarity between the travellers, lies in the fact they provide the same opportunity for adventure and self-discovery by engaging with the landscape. De Maistre's, however, is more "practical for those who were not as brave and wealthy" allowing ordinary people, possibly like the reader, or those who are "poor" or "afraid" or have a fear of danger, to have a safer course. The exploratory language of "spies" and "complex" refers to his bed but the emotional response gained from this landscape is a memory of the "calm" and "pleasant reveries" experienced there. The use of a connective "And" to begin the next paragraph reflects the informality and unconsciousness of this experience and the challenge that even the insignificant is of importance if one knows how to look at it.

This brings the reader to possibly one of the core purposes of the text , the importance of mental rather than physical outlook as in, "dependent of the mindset...rather than the destination...". The questioning of whether the local landscape is as important as the juxtaposed high mountains of the Humboldt expedition- is shown through the use of the double negative when describing the bedroom as "no-less" interesting. This shows how the safe can provide as much opportunity for personal growth as the adventurous. The reader is included in this conversation through the use of rhetorical question.

De Botton's use of anecdote, specifically the explanation of his own attempt at the De Maistre-like travel experience, leads to the development of the reader's ability to see opportunities in all landscapes. His bedroom, as the photograph attests or gives proof of, is unrealistic as a place of travel, so he moves to the neighbourhood. On his journey he attempts to truly engage with the landscape around him and be open to the complexity rather than the simplified list. To do this he identifies a range of perspectives and elements. Each item is explained; a bus, the weather, the number of people, traffic. De Botton reacts against his natural "sensitivity" and reduces this new landscape to a small number of elements ensuring effective interaction. The lyrical complexity of the sentence structure " A bus ...outside invisible", which makes the unnoticeable visible, and "The power of my primary goal... Georgian, Edwardian and Victorian, architecture along a single block", reveals the historical beauty of a small area through looking at the "layers of value" which are exposed. This process was difficult and took concentration but eventually led to growth and "began to bear fruit."

Concluding, de Botton shows his own development, through the use of first person "I" statement again but with a change to "I reflected, I tried, I liked" rather than the "I had" at the beginning. This development of emotions reflects the individual's ability to relate to the landscape. The dichotomy that we are challenged with as readers throughout the text, is to find a balance between the "boring daily life" and the "marvellous world". The concluding message from de Botton is that we do not have to travel to escape the chaos and clutter of our daily lives but that we do need to try and notice what we have already seen around us.

SUGGESTED RELATED TEXTS

Mockumentary

An Idiot Abroad – Ricky Gervais 2010-13 Television series

Film

Amelie - Film, 2001. Dir Jean-Pierre Jeunet

A Good Year - Film, 2006. Dir Ridley Scott

A Passage to India, 1984. Dir David Lean. Also novel by EM Forster.

Eat Pray Love – Film by Elizabeth Gilbert. 2007, Bloomsbury. There is also a written, memoir version.

Lost in Translation - Film, 2003. Dir Sofia Coppola

Midnight in Paris - Film, 2011. Dir Woody Allen

Shirley Valentine - Film, 1989. Dir Willy Russell

The Beach - Film, 2000. Dir Danny Boyle.

The Best Exotic Marigold Hotel (One and Two) - Film, 2012 and 2015 sequel. Dir John Madden.

Under the Tuscan Sun - Film, 2003. Dir Audrey Wells

Up in the Air - Film, 2009. Dir Jason Reitman

Fiction – Short Stories, Novels

Burial Rites – by Hannah Kent. Little, Brown and Company, 2013. Speculative biography, set in Iceland.)

Into the Wild - by J Krakauer, later a film. Anchor, 1997.

Island: The Complete Stories - by Alistair Macleod, published by McClelland and Stewart, 2000.

Kitchen – by Banana Yoshimoto, published by Grove Press 2006. First published 1988.

Like Water for Chocolate – by Laura Esquivel. Anchor, 1995.

Northanger Abbey – by Jane Austen. +First published 1818. (This is classed as an early Gothic novel. Gothic novels are meant to evoke fear, through representations of place.)

Perfume – by Patrick Suskind, 1985. Historical, cross-genre novel. First published in German.

Persepolis – Marjan Satrapi an autobiographical graphic novel Pantheon, 2004. - in English (first published 2000).

The God of Small Things – by Arundhati Roy, published by Random House, 1997.

The Merry-go Round in the Sea – by Randolph Stow, Penguin 2013. First published 1965.(Australian)

The Poisonwood Bible – by Barbara Kingsolver, published by Harper Collins, 1998.

The Road – by Cormac Mc Carthy. AA Knopf, 2006. A dystopian journey novel.

The Secret Life of Walter Milly - by James Thurber. A Short Story and now film. First published in *The New Yorker* on March 19, 1939.

The Secret River – by Kate Grenville. Text Publishing. 2005. (Australian)

The Shipping News – by E. Annie Proulx, published by Charles Scribner's Sons, 1993.

Twelve Edminston Street - by David Malouf. Penguin, 1986. A return to the author's childhood home in Brisbane

Non-Fiction

Appointment Northwest – by Peter Skrzynecki, Five Senses Publications, 2014.

My Place – by Sally Morgan. Fremantle Press, 1987.

Night - by Elie Weisel, 2006. (Translated by M. Weisel) Autobiographical account of time spent as a teenager in Nazi Death Camps.

Persepolis – Marjan Satrapi an autobiographical graphic novel Pantheon, 2004. - in English (first published 2000).

The Orchard – Drusilla Modjeska, Macmillan, 1994.

The Journals of Explorers could also be considered and used as related texts.

Play

Our Town – Thornton Wilder. First produced 1938. Harper Collins 2014.

The Crucible – by Arthur Miller, 1953. Consider the setting of Salem and the context. The landscape will by necessity involove the moral and religious feeling of the town and perhaps be informed by the Macarthyism of the time of writing. Representation in a dramatic form can be seen through characterisation, costuming, stage settings and so on. Directors can make additional choices.

Summer of the Seventeenth Doll – by Ray Lawler. First produced in 1976-77.

Under Milkwood. A Play for Voices. Dylan Thomas. First produced 1954.

Picture Books

A Bush Christening – A. B Paterson, Illust Q Hole. Angus and Robertson. 1996.

Remembering Lionsville - by Bronwyn Bancroft. Allen and Unwin, 2013.

Ice, Wind, Rock Douglas Mawson in the Antarctic – by Peter Gouldthorpe. Lothian, 2013.

Poetry

Elizabeth Bishop – US poet d 1979. She explores the concept of 'Geographical mirrors'.

TS ELiot – Modernist poets such as Eliot connected people and places with a bleak pessimism. This was a reaction to the post WW1 era as such writers often saw the futility and pity brought by The Great War.

Seamus Heaney – An Irish poet whose poems often deal with Irish peasant farmers.

Keats – A Romantic poet. Other Romantic poets were also concerned with people and places. They saw place inspiring emotions and reflecting the Divine.

Pablo Neruda – Chilean poet and politician.

Peter Skrzynecki – An Australian poet with a Polish/Ukranian heritage. Look at '10 Mary Street' and 'Felix Skrzynecki.'

THE ESSAY

The essay has been the subject of numerous texts and you should have the basic form well in hand. As teachers, the point we would emphasise would be to link the paragraphs both to each other and back to your argument (which should directly respond to the question). Of course, ensure your argument is logical and sustained.

Make sure you use specific examples and that your quotes are accurate. To ensure that you respond to the question make sure you plan carefully and are sure what relevant point each paragraph is making. It is solid technique to actually 'tie up' each point by explicitly coming back to the question.

When composing an essay the basic conventions of the form are:

- State your argument, outline the points to be addressed and perhaps have a brief definition.

↓

A solid structure for each paragraph is:

- Topic sentence (*the main idea and its link to the previous paragraph/ argument*)
- Explanation / discussion of the point including links between texts if applicable.
- Detailed evidence (*Close textual reference- quotes, incidents and technique discussion.*)
- Tie up by restating the point's relevance to argument / question

↓

- Summary of points
- Final sentence that restates your argument

As well as this basic structure you will need to focus on:

Audience – The audience for the essay the audience must be considered formal unless specifically stated otherwise. Therefore,= your language must reflect the audience. This gives you the opportunity to use the jargon and vocabulary that you have learnt in English. For the audience ensure your introduction is clear and has impact. Avoid slang or colloquial language including contractions (like doesn't, eg., etc.).

Purpose – The purpose of the essay is to answer the question given. The examiner evaluates how well you can make an argument and understand the module's issues and its text(s). An essay is solidly structured so its composer can analyse ideas. This is where you earn marks. It does not retell the story or state the obvious.

Communication – Take a few minutes to plan the essay. If you rush into your answer it is almost certain you will not make the most of the brief 40 minutes to show all you know about the question. More likely you will include irrelevant details that do not gain you marks but waste your precious time. Remember an essay is formal so **do not** do the following: story-tell, list and number points, misquote, use slang or colloquial language, be vague, use non sentences or fail to address the question.

How have composers in this elective shaped your understanding of the relationship between people and landscapes?

In your response refer closely to your prescribed text and one related text.

The composers in this elective have helped to shape my understanding of the relationship between people and landscapes. Alain de Botton's non-fiction text *The Art of Travel* (2002), in particular the chapter 'On Curiosity' shows the excitement and joy that can be derived from experiencing dangerous landscapes. Mary Shelley's 1818 novel, *Frankenstein* further reveals Romantic sentiments in the comfort and solace that natural landscapes afford both Victor and the monster. Alain de Botton's 'On Travelling Places' shows how a landscape that may initially seem depressing can, in fact, paradoxically allow responders to feel comfort and connection.

De Botton presents the story of Humboldt, an individual who is challenged and stimulated by his landscape. The landscape inspires Humboldt's drive, ambition and his curiosity. De Botton substantiates this with a direct quote from Humboldt, where he outlines how the study of maps and travel books 'aroused in me a secret fascination that was, at times, almost irresistible.'

De Botton peppers the description of the landscapes Humboldt experiences with luscious visual imagery, enticing the reader and capturing their imagination with an unspoilt terrain. Details such as 'The hills of calcareous rock on which the town stood were dotted with cacti and opuntia, their trunks branching out like candelabras coated with lichen,' are beautifully crafted, utilising similes to create an exotic, yet elegant atmosphere, where the physical creations of man have a symbiotic relationship with nature. In this landscape, man and nature have again become one. De Botton highlights the perfection and unity of man and nature when curiosity allows an individual to be led to new discoveries.

He also creates a sense of danger, excitement and adventure when detailing Humboldt's expeditions. For instance he directly quotes Humboldt's account of one of his expeditions to show the joy and thrill that can be obtained when experiencing a landscape for the first time. Humboldt recounts 'we were constantly climbing through clouds...the ridge was not wider than eight or ten inches...On the right lay a fearful abyss.' Here, the use of emotive language coupled with the descriptive visual imagery creates a mood of imaginative wonder. It stimulates fear as Humboldt experiences risk in a foreign landscape. De Botton shows readers how landscapes can bring much joy, beauty and excitement when experiences both first hand and vicariously.

Mary Shelley's fictional text *Frankenstein* also details how one can derive joy from a particular landscape. Victor's interaction with the landscape allows him to momentarily forget his creation of the 'monster' and the feelings of despondency that have followed him after this act. The thunderstorm that Victor encounters "burst with a terrific crash over [his] head. It was echoed from Saleve, the Juras, and the Alps of Savoy; vivid flashes of lightning dazzled [his] eyes, illuminating the lake, making it appear like a vast sheet of fire; then for an instant everything seemed of a pitchy darkness, until the eye recovered itself from the preceding flash". Here, the multi-sensory imagery shows how Victor finds the storm to be a powerful influence on his emotions and psychology. This can also be seen through his use of the adverb 'so' when describing that he finds this landscape "so beautiful yet terrific" that it "elevat[es]

[his] spirits". Furthermore, the landscape helps to ease some of Victor's grief. During Victor's family trip to the Arveiron, "these sublime and magnificent scenes afforded [him] the greatest consolation that [he was] capable of receiving. They elevated [him] from all littleness of feeling; and although they did not remove [his] grief, they subdued and tranquillized it" Similarly, Victor remembers "the effect that the view of [Montanvert's] tremendous and ever-moving glacier had produced upon [his] mind. It had filled him with a sublime ecstasy that gave wings to the soul, and allowed it to soar from the obscure world to light and joy". Here the metaphor outlines the freedom and joy that Victor experiences from the landscape. For Victor, "the sight of the awful and majestic in nature had indeed always the effect of solemnizing [his] mind, and caus[ed] [him] to forget the passing cares of life" Therefore, it is Victor's powerful experience with the sublime landscape that allows him momentary comfort and joy, before the reappearance of his creature has him submerged into misery, guilt and regret once more.

In contrast to the previous sublime natural landscapes, de Botton explores the powerful and momentary impact something as mundane as a service station can have on the individual psyche. De Botton suggests that 'architecturally miserable' man-made spaces can offer a sense of connection, comfort and 'reflection' for those feeling lonely and isolated. Initially, de Botton observes how 'The geographical isolation [of the service station] enforced the atmosphere of solitude in the dining area. The lighting was unforgiving, bringing out pallor and blemishes. The chairs and seats, painted in childishly bright colours had the strained jollity of a fake smile.' Here the repeated use of sentences beginning with the definite article 'the' has the effect of listing and creating a sense of sterility and hollowness through its description of objects. The audience imagines an artificial environment lacking in authenticity and depth of meaning and the effect is to find it repulsive, distancing and uninspiring. However, de Botton cleverly subverts the audience's response by personally reflecting on how such an environment could, in fact, erase extreme feelings of loneliness and generate an understanding in the individual that they are not alone. De Botton states that his experience of the service station was in fact a transformative one, 'I felt lonely, but for once this was a gentle, even pleasant kind of loneliness, rather than unfolding against a backdrop of laughter and fellowship, in which I would suffer from a contrast between my mood and the environment, it had its locus in a place where everyone was a stranger, where the difficulties of communication and the frustrated longing for love seemed to be acknowledged and brutally celebrated by the architecture and the writing.' This very long sentence captures the overwhelming impact that the landscape of the service station had on de Botton erasing a range of debilitating emotions such as desperate loneliness, suffering and frustration.

Therefore, the composers de Botton and Shelley have helped to shape my understanding of the relationship between people and landscapes. Alain de Botton's non-fiction text *The Art of Travel* (2002), in particular the chapter 'On Curiosity' shows the excitement and joy that can be derived from experiencing dangerous natural landscapes. Mary Shelley's *Frankenstein* further shows how one can often find comfort and solace in natural landscapes, whilst Alain de Botton's 'On Travelling Places' shows how a landscape that may initially seem sad and miserable can in fact paradoxically evoke feelings of comfort and connection.

(Students could further develop these ideas, add additional aspects to the introduction and develop these in the main body of the essay. For example, the module's focus on text and representation alerts candidates to focus on how the connections between people and place are depicted in various text types. Non-fiction texts will convey personal accounts whereas novels will describe, using strong imagery, the connections between characters and places and the effects place may have on people. Context may also be relevant as in the case of Shelley who conveys aspects of the Romantic era thinking regarding the restorative power of nature. Urban landscapes are more likely to be depicted in a bleak fashion by Modernist composers such as the poet TS Eliot.)

Sample HSC Style Questions

The following are Module C Representation and Text sample essay questions which have been shaped to the elective, 'Representing People and Landscapes'.

1

'At the heart of representation are acts of deliberate selection and emphasis.'

Do the texts you have studied demonstrate this in relation to 'Representing People and Landscapes'?

Refer to your prescribed text and at least TWO other related texts of your own choosing.

2

Texts in this elective offer perspectives on the significance of landscape in human experiences.

Were you persuaded to embrace these perspectives? Refer to your prescribed text and at least TWO other related texts of your own choosing.

3

How have the texts studied in this elective challenged your ways of thinking about 'Representing People and Landscapes' ?

Make detailed reference to your prescribed text and at least ONE other related text of your own choosing.

4

Compare how the texts you have studied emphasise the complexities evident in the relationship between people and landscapes. In your response, refer to your prescribed text and at least ONE other related text of your own choosing.

5

Analyse the ways in which the relationship between people and landscapes generates diverse and provocative insights.

In your response, make detailed reference to your prescribed text and at least ONE other related text of your own choosing.

6

To what extent has textual form shaped your understanding of people and their relationship with the landscape?

In your response, make detailed reference to your prescribed text and at least ONE other related text of your own choosing.

7

Explore how *The Art of Travel* and ONE other related text of your own choosing represent the relationship between people and landscapes in unique and evocative ways.

8

Analyse how the representation of people and landscapes leads us to a greater awareness of the complexity of human attitudes and behaviour.

In your response, make detailed reference to your prescribed text and at least ONE other related text of your own choosing.

9

'All representations are acts of manipulation.'

To what extent does your study of Representing People and Landscapes support this statement? In your response, make detailed reference to your prescribed text and ONE other related text of your own choosing.

Non-Essay Style Questions

Remember that you can also be asked to write in a form other than an essay. Ensure you revise writing in a variety of text types.

For example, 'Imagine you have a radio show titled, Representation and Text. You are recording an episode called, Representing People and Landscape, Exploring Links in Texts. You have invited de Botton as well as two other composers to be guests in your panel discussion.

Write the interview.

REFERENCES

Board of Studies NSW *HSC English Prescriptions 2015-2020*

HTTP://WWW.BOARDOFSTUDIES.NSW.EDU.AU/SYLLABUS_HSC/ENGLISH/ENG-STD-ADV-PRESCRIPTIONS-2015-20.HTML

UK National Statistics,

HTTP://WWW.ONS.GOV.UK/ONS/REL/OTT/TRAVEL-TRENDS/2002/INDEX.HTML

World Trade Organisation *Tourism Services*

HTTPS://WWW.WTO.ORG/ENGLISH/TRATOP_E/SERV_E/W51.DOC

De Botton, Alain. *The Art of Travel* Random House, 2002.

Shelley, Mary Wollstonecraft. *Frankenstein or, The Modern Prometheus*. Berkeley and Los Angeles: University of California Press, 1984.

RELATED TEXTS

Honi Soit Qui Mal Y Pense- T Abood. Short Film

This four minute film tells the story of a common humanity, regardless of setting. It recounts a soldier's appreciation for Australia, his homeland. It was a Tropfest winner.

When the Wind Blows – Raymond Briggs. Picture Book

Once an HSC text, this wonderful story shows the effect of an instantaneous change in the landscape and how it affects one couple. Hilda and James have their lives disrupted when an atomic war breaks out and destroys everything. Their simple naivety is in direct contrast to the effects on their environment. Poignant and relevant. Done in cartoon strip style.

Heart of Darkness – Joseph Conrad. Novel

A novella that shows how a landscape can permanently alter an individual's response to the world. A civilised man enters the Congolese jungle and becomes far more strange than those he went to protect. The jungle overtakes him and the famous line 'The horror, the horror' emanates from his change. For those looking for something with less reading you can try the film version which changes the time and bases the narrative line in the Vietnam War. Try Francis Ford Coppola's film *Apocalypse Now.*

I Heard the Owl Call my Name - Margaret Craven. Novel

This text tells of a young Anglican minister named Mark Brian who has not long to live. He learns about life when he is to be sent to a parish in British Columbia. he learns from the native Indians and their relationship with the land. it is an old text but was on the top seller list for many years and still has a lot to say about people, values and landscapes.

The Island - Armin Greder. Picture Book

This picture book is a bleak reminder about being different and the impact of an outsider on a closed landscape; the island. The man who lands is alienated because of unnatural fears. The islanders then shut themselves off by building walls around the island so no one can arrive unexpectedly, again. Great graphics complement the harsh words of rejection.

Snow Falling on Cedars by David Guterson. Novel

A moving crime-fiction narrative that is set on San Piedro Island, a fictional place in Puget Sound. The characters are tied intimately to the landscape which offers both solace and hardship in its own way. The descriptions of the landscape are sensitive and sympathetic to nature as are those in the set text. Lonliness and conflict are key themes.

Peripheral Light – John Kinsella

The poet Kinsella creates a landscape through words. The poetry is based on first-hand experience, observation, imagination with a specific number of intellectual focuses. He contrasts in many of the poems in this collection the rugged, natural beauty and the imposed landscape with the problems it brings. Excellent for examining dichotomy in landscape and people's views on that landscape.

Jindabyne – Ray Lawrence

A sinister murder in the Australian bush and caught up in it are four fishermen who let the body stay in the water rather than disrupt their fishing trip. To make matters worse she is an Aboriginal girl and the race issue becomes another aspect. The film is not about the murder but rather about the characters and the response they have to the trouble. The Australian landscape is integral to the characters and we do get, in the conclusion, the Aboriginal aspect of attachment to the land.

A Passage to India – Dir. David Lean.+ Film version. E M Forster (Novel)

The tale of Miss Adela Quested who leaves the rain soaked greenery of England to find a new life in India with her proposed fiancé, Ronnie Heslop. She finds India extraordinary and causes some conflict with the local natives and the British with her interest in the local people. After all this she returns to Britain a very changed woman. The spectacular Indian continent is the star of the film and its impact on the characters is the central issue.

***The Chronicles of Narnia* – C. S. Lewis. Novel**

You may have already read one of these where the children are transported into the imaginative landscape of Narnia where the children are royalty and lead the people to freedom over the evil witch. Briefly, good for illustrating how landscape can alter the perception of individuals and groups, changing how they are also perceived and how they respond.

***Island* – Alistair MacLeod. Short Stories**

One of the best collections of short stories ever – if not the best, especially for people and landscapes. MacLeod explores the landscape of Cape Breton, its Gaelic culture, the fishing and mining history and how the setting impacts on all this in a sympathetic, stylish manner. Any of the superb stories would be a great choice.

Highly recommended.

***Fly Away Peter* – David Malouf. Novel**

In the short novel Malouf imagines a vast landscape that covers two worlds and blends them uniquely, linked by the protagonist, Jim. From the stunning beauty of the Queensland coast to the realistic landscape of the war, Malouf shows the wonder of nature and the cost of war. Life in the trenches, the innocence and knowledge of nature make the earth a symbol.

'Memory: how people remember the landscape'

Geraldine Mate. Article

This excellent article discusses specifically the integration of people and landscape. See an example paragraph below.

> *'The markers of how we remember in the landscape seem to be everywhere. The reminders of the 1974 flood, or even the 1893 flood, sneak up and are found in unexpected places like the rafters of a picnic shelter. Park names proclaim the stories of prominent or well-regarded members of local communities. The markers of loss - a cross and a posy of flowers marking the place of yet another fatal car accident involving a young person - appear at otherwise unremarkable points along the highway. Why do we mark these spots in this way? It is perhaps a reminder, a warning to others to drive more carefully, take it slower around the corners; to be wary of floods. But these markers are also focal points for remembering - whether of people or events, big or small.'*

HTTP://WWW.QHATLAS.COM.AU/ESSAY/MEMORY-HOW-PEOPLE-REMEMBER-LANDSCAPE

The View From Castle Rock **– Alice Munro. Novel**

This novel is about a rural Scottish place, poor and isolated. A family uproot from their rural life and head to America for a completely new landscape and life. Even the sea when on ship needs adaptation from them all. They end up happy in Canada West. Here the thrust is about imagining what can happen in a new landscape after the old offers nothing.

Where the Wild Things Are **- Maurice Sendak. Picture Book**

A picture book that is regarded as a classic. A small boy journeys through an imaginative landscape where he becomes king of the 'wild things' before returning home. Well worth a look because of its status as an all-time favourite. It shows landscape and imagination.

***Night Street* – Kristel Thornell. Novel** Here is a novel set in Australia about a fictional character 'Clarice' but based on the real Clarice Beckett, a historical figure in the Australian art world. Here we see the artist's landscape and the manner in which it shapes her. Her life is determined by her art and the way she sees the world also. A very personal account of landscape and people.

YouTube

For those inclined to the visual for their materials try typing people and landscapes into the search engine. There are some very interesting visually creative videos that people have posted. One example is a video of Algeria: People and landscapes found at:

HTTPS://WWW.YOUTUBE.COM/WATCH?V=2AX-ASJ1KYM

Another more propagandist video is at

HTTPS://WWW.YOUTUBE.COM/WATCH?V=5B-MFIWFDQM

which is a study of New Mexico people and landscapes that highlights people interacting with the landscape. Listen for the song in the background.